ISBN 978-1-331-03297-7
PIBN 10136040

1 MONTH OF FREE READING

at

www.ForgottenBooks.com

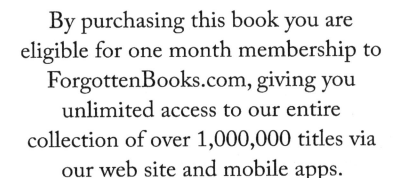

By purchasing this book you are eligible for one month membership to ForgottenBooks.com, giving you unlimited access to our entire collection of over 1,000,000 titles via our web site and mobile apps.

To claim your free month visit:

www.forgottenbooks.com/free136040

English
Français
Deutsche
Italiano
Español
Português

www.forgottenbooks.com

Mythology Photography **Fiction**
Fishing Christianity **Art** Cooking
Essays Buddhism Freemasonry
Medicine **Biology** Music **Ancient**
Egypt Evolution Carpentry Physics
Dance Geology **Mathematics** Fitness
Shakespeare **Folklore** Yoga Marketing
Confidence Immortality Biographies
Poetry **Psychology** Witchcraft
Electronics Chemistry History **Law**
Accounting **Philosophy** Anthropology
Alchemy Drama Quantum Mechanics
Atheism Sexual Health **Ancient History**
Entrepreneurship Languages Sport
Paleontology Needlework Islam
Metaphysics Investment Archaeology
Parenting Statistics Criminology
Motivational

THE LOVE OF HELOISE AND
ABELARD

E LOVE

ELOISE AND ABELARD

POEM

M. RUDLAND

DON : KEGAN PAUL, TRENCH
BNER & CO.

In singing the manifold excellences of love, I have endeavoured to tell of what, at first entirely passionate, has become ennobled by its own repression, and there is no example so notable as the story of Heloise and Abelard for my illustration.

It is in the assurance of the ennobling influence of love, and the full knowledge that success, happiness, and existence are alike dependent upon its issues, that I inscribe to you these verses.

870384

HELOISE

Ἀ μεγάλα μοι Κύπρις ἔθ' ἡβώοντι παρέστα
νηπίαχον τὸν Ἔρωτα καλᾶς ἐκ χειρὸς ἄγοισα
ἐς χθόνα νευστάζοντα, τόσον δέ μοι ἔφρασε μῦθον·
μέλπειν μοι φίλε βῶτα λαβὼν τὸν Ἔρωτα δίδασκε.
ὣς λέγε· χἀ μὲν ἀπῆνθεν· ἐγὼ δ' ὅσα βωκολίασδον,
νήπιος, ὡς ἐθέλοντα μαθεῖν τὸν Ἔρωτα δίδασκον,
ὡς εὗρεν πλαγίαυλον ὁ Πάν, ὡς αὐλὸν Ἀθάνα,
ὡς χέλυν Ἑρμάων, κιθάραν ὡς ἁδέ' Ἀπόλλων.
ταῦτά νιν ἐξεδίδασκον· ὁ δ' οὐκ ἐμπάζετο μύθων,
ἀλλά μοι αὐτὸς ἄειδεν ἐρωτύλα, καί μ' ἐδίδασκεν
θνατῶν ἀθανάτων τε πόθους καὶ ματέρος ἔργα.
κἠγὼν ἐκλαθόμαν μὲν ὅσων τὸν Ἔρωτα δίδασκον,
ὅσσα δ' Ἔρως μ' ἐδίδαξεν ἐρωτύλα πάντ' ἐδιδάχθην.

—BION.

Tutti li miei pensier parlan d'amore.—DANTE.

Στᾶθι κἄντα φίλος . . . ˙
καὶ τὰν ἐπ' ὄσσοις ἀμπέτασον χάριν.—SAPPHO.

. Τὸ μέλημα τοὐμόν.—SAPPHO.

I SING dear songs of memories that are dead,
    Great songs of consolation to be sung
    While all the tendons of my heart are wrung,
Till in my singing I am comfortéd.

God hath from the beginning willed it so ;
    I love thee Abelard, and do confess
    The passion and the wond'rous tenderness
Which from the founts of love divinely flow.

For we were drawn together to our birth,
    And all along the ages, of a truth,
    Have moved to the glad meeting of our youth
That made our twin souls one upon the earth :

That made us very one, Belovéd.   Long
    Have I lost e'en my inmost thought in thee,
    And count thee more than any heaven in fee,
And loving, know not any right or wrong.

Nay ! Abelard, I could not do thee wrong ;
 I greet thee with a reverent trembling love
 That slays itself below, that it may prove
More wonderful hereafter and more strong.

For though we walk apart and love hath dearth,
 Love's song I will go singing through the gloom :
 The while the flowers lose something of their bloom,
And there is less of sunshine on the earth.

It is the New Year's morning, and I pray
 For blessings on dear Abelard, whose name
 Doth flood my being always with the flame
That leaps to his dear spirit every way.

I make no other prayer to God on high,
 Nor can I, might I, add one other word :
 Only " God bless thee, Abelard," is heard
Always by all the angels ceaselessly.

The rosary I hold in trembling hand
 Is worn away with Abelard's dear round,
 While evensong and matin always sound
The name of Abelard. And the command

"Take this in my remembrance," at the feast,
  I take with him in spirit at my side.
  "With Abelard," I murmur, and abide
Long after the priest's minist'ring hath ceased.

Belovéd, when I look into thine eyes—
  I see them in my vision every night
  Upwelling in old wonder and delight—
I know that thou hast looked on Paradise.

Belovéd, I have looked into thy face,
  And I shall never be as heretofore,
  Because my soul desires thee evermore:
May love's sustaining guardians give me grace.

Thine eyes have drawn my soul out through mine eyes.
  Belovéd, thou hast robbed me of my soul.
  No part thereof thou takest, but the whole
That thou requitest in love's Paradise.

For I have drawn thy soul in fair exchange,
  I saw thee yield it, Dearest, in thy gaze.
  Clearly I saw it through the gathering haze,
So wonderful love's power is and so strange.

Belovéd, if love ever be a sin,
    I would not change my sin for any place
    Where white garbed saints look palely on each face
And cold wide eyes lack any love therein.

With all the deep dear passion of my love,
    I dream of thee, Belovéd, through the night,
    And clasp thee as of old with the delight
That first our mutual souls did swiftly move.

Belov'd, I will be passionate, I know
    Thou wast, nay! art as passionate as I.
    And surely shall they chide me tenderly,
Who glean in the great harvest love doth sow.

I praise God for thy love anew each day:
    And nought but love remember or recall,
    Because thou art my veriest all in all,
In waking time and sleeping, and alway.

For in the dark, clear-written as in flame,
    My sleeping eyes are dazzled with a light
    That breaks in clearest vision on my sight
With all the sweet dear letters of thy name.

I kiss the " A " for love's acknowledgment,
    The " B " for all the blessing of thy love,
    And " E " for the eternities to prove,
And " L " that is as love's own lineament.—

I kiss the " A " that marks love's sweet ascent,
    And " R " for all the raiment of love's room,
    And " D " that has the dominance o'er doom,
Because it is thy name's dear complement.

And when, from where the oriel window dips,
    The red sun leaps into the amorous sky,
    And streams upon my slumbers as I lie,
I wake with thy sweet name upon my lips.

Should this be otherwise, thou being thou,
    And I, being made as I am ?   Dearest, nay !
    So sweet my waking should be everyday ;
I praise heaven for my love's deep passion now.

When Abelard, thou looked'st in mine eyes,
    And I in thine, Belovéd, and in each
    Was love that leaped to love, outwinging speech
In silence, awe, and wisting sweet surmise :

And our two souls rose startled from the deep,
    And looked on each and read love's sacred sign,
    And knew the other wond'rous and divine,
Arisen and fresh from immemorial sleep:

O golden splendour of love's perfect dawn !
    What day was e'er as that day, my Belov'd,
    Whereto the ages and all things were moved?
That our two souls in harmony were drawn:

When looking in each other's eyes we knew
    Love's perfect power made manifestly lord,
    And bowed before the presence of the word,
And stood with the soul's wonder streaming through.

The love in lovers' eyes is as a sail
    That glistens in the golden glow, and brings
    The loved one with the heart's own whisperings,
When sweetly the soft winds of love prevail.

In whitest comb the golden honey gleams,
    So doth the love, Belovéd, in thy glance.
    Scarce may I look upon thy countenance
Because my soul desires thee in my dreams.

Methought that thou did'st look upon me, Dear,
    And from afar thine Heloise behold.
    So Love in swift communion is foretold,
So leaped my heart within me, " He is here."

I saw thee not, Belovéd.   Nay ! before
    Thou cam'st e'en nigh the portal ; unaware,
    My heart, by its rejoicing, did declare
The sovereign form it worships evermore.

For true love needs not vision, neither speech ;
    But swiftly leaps from soul to soul like flame.
    And high beyond all knowledge and all name,
Transcends the wond'rous mysteries it doth teach.

Oh ! who shall name my love a sin in me,
    Who love thee only and am bounden thrall,
    And know not any praise or blame at all,
But only one surpassing love of thee ?

One love that is all heaven all my days :
    My heaven, my crown, my joy, my every breath ;
    That leaps, exults, and shouts, and laughs at death,
And is life's one abiding song of praise.

I took a book, Belovéd, from its place,
 Because it had been thine, wherein was writ,
 Each letter a pure pearl with radiance lit,
The circlet of thy name's sufficing grace,

And two sweet words—but two.—Thy childish hand
 Had written "with love" "with love" across the
  page:
 First tokens of life's lordliest heritage,
That even the coldest heart might understand.

So doth thy first love come to me anew.
 Surely in worlds before us it was born,
 And swayed about the earth until the morn
The eyes it lit remembered love and knew.

Great lovers that have loved of old, and sought
 Through heaven, through hell, through earth, your
  proper mate,
 Now surely are ye all compassionate
For Abelard and me together brought.

For love hath no regret, whatever chance,
 I love—let the sufficing words be said.
 I love—and therefore am I comfortéd,
Nor fear I any change nor tarriance.

Love knows not shame but glories in its bliss,
    And doth confront a world of men unmoved.
    So blessed 'tis to love and to be loved,
O come, my Love, I greet thee with a kiss.

Come now, ye sweet companions of my love,
    Dark Sappho of the burning fire of song;
    And thou, Orpheus, thy melodies prolong,
And tune upon the viol that I prove.

O Cupid, son of Venus, pluck the string,
    And sing of thy sweet Psyche, with refrain
    Heard ever o'er the noise of mortal pain,
Because love hath so sweet imagining.

O Venus, radiant queen of love's delight,
    O guardian of th' imperishable fire,
    That smil'st upon the flames of my desire,
Be with me in my tenderest dreams to-night.

And passionate with arms around thee flung,
    Lost Cleopatra of the lustrous south,
    Who pantest with hot kisses on thy mouth,
O tell me how true lovers' songs are sung.

O kingly son, O David, swell the praise
>Of love beyond all mortal love, and roll
>The perfected companionship of soul,
Immortally commemorate with thy lays.

I sing the dear dear sacrifice of love,
>For true love loves the giving, and to give
>To the belovéd is new life to live,
That is beyond earth's guerdon and above.

I sing of all the sweet desire of love,
>Belovéd, I desire thee.   Verily
>Thou know'st that thou art heaven itself to me,
Who only and who always to thee move.

I sing of all love's manifold consent,
>And whatso thou desirest, I desire,
>And greet thee always with the answering fire
That brightly flameth in love's firmament.

I sing of truest faith that lovers keep,
>For love can never falter nor deceive.
>And whosoe'er loves truly doth believe,
And doth love's golden confidences reap.

For love hath hope on earth and sees afar—
    And always is its banner overhead—
    It hath nor fear nor burden, but doth tread
In certainty and sureness as a star.

And love is one with truth and cannot lie,
    And cannot do a hurt or any wrong,
    Therefore by all the angels are there sung
The praises of true lovers constantly.

And love is seen all beautiful, and hath
    Sweet aspect in the night time and the day,
    And shines about men's vision every way,
And leaves the years all glorious in its path.

Belovéd, when I look into the night,
    And see my seven stars gleaming in the sky,
    I know that the north star is told thereby,
So love within thine eyes is by love's light.

Oh ! vainly do I scan the barren walls,
    And seek my soul's belovéd every day,
    And " surely he is coming," softly say,
And turn upon my pathway through the halls.

O thou, my soul so loveth, come to me.
    The song birds know the singing time is come,
    And chirp and twitter round their fibred home,
And only I am riven apart from thee.

Upon the starry canopy is writ
    What was from the beginning, and doth blend
    So surely unto the appointed end,
That angels cannot change a word of it.

How sweet a name is love upon the lips,
    How beautifully written in the looks,
    O lovers ! that forswear all other books,
Forswear not the eternal manuscript.

How precious is the word upon the ears ;
    O rhythm swoll'n into one perfect song,
    The hymn divine for evermore prolong,
Until the ardent lord of love appears.

For I, that would renounce love, sing love's praise,
    So am I fast made prisoner, and in thrall
    Sing only how that love is all in all,
And bow upon the altar love doth raise.

Till, Abelard, thou cam'st into my life,
 And thrilled'st my soul with being that might live,
 My life was as a wounded fugitive,
That prayeth for the falling of death's knife.

Nay! life was as the empty glass that yields
 New torture in the agonies of thirst.
 So silently I held my days accurst,
Because the vines grew barren in my fields.

For love is the rich wine, and love is life,
 Love is all things, Belovéd, Love is fame,
 'Tis length of years, and every sweetest name,
And wealth and peace, how great soe'er the strife.

And whoso' liveth without love is dead,
 And who hath not known love, whate'er he be,
 Is lesser than all lovers. Verily!
Only by love is life seen perfectéd.

For learning is but weariness, and fame
 All vanity and hollowness within.
 And gold, the broidered coat to wrap men in
Veils not the soul's nobility nor shame.

For man is but the man, whate'er he seem,
    And woman is the woman, and the dress
    Adds not, and takes not from the loveliness ;
Love sees with clearer vision than ye dream.

Love sees with clearest vision.   'Tis not blind.
    O fools ! love sees from the eternities
    The beauty and the goodliness, that is
The aspect of the all-pervading mind.

LOVE'S RENUNCIATION

The heart knoweth his own bitterness.—Proverbs xiv. 10.

I go to prove my soul !
I see my way as birds their trackless way.
I shall arrive ! what time, what circuit first,
I ask not : but unless God send his hail
Or blinding fireballs, sleet or stifling snow,
In some time, his good time, I shall arrive :
He guides me and the bird.   In his good time !
—ROBERT BROWNING.

BELOVÉD, must I win love's very crown,
  Must I renounce thee, my Belovéd? Nay!
  Forgive me, for the word is hard to say,
Nor may I take up love who lay love down.

'Tis done, 'tis done. See are mine eyes not dry?
  I shall not see thee, hear thee, any more.
  Nor read in thy dear writing o'er and o'er,
"Surely I come to see thee presently."

Think not, Belovéd, memory shall fade
  Of what thou wast to Heloise; her lord,
  Her master, and as God's own very word,
For ever to be worshipped and obeyed.

Must love slay love, Belovéd? It is hard.
  Nay! love is not so pitiless to forego
  The transports that true lovers only know.
Oh! spare my love unto me, Abelard.

I may lose thee, Belovéd, but not love.
    Nay! take not memory from me with love's spell;
    Love knows no fear of any heaven or hell,
It is too deep abiding and above.

Love must be very patient, Love, always;
    For love hath great desire, and love hath more
    That doth redeem love from desire.   Therefore
My love doth slay its love and give God praise.

I do renounce thee, Love, I give thee o'er,
    Because it is thy good that I desire.
    What ails it that my heart shall break or tire
With memories but for nurture evermore?

Yea! for the light hath gone from out mine eyes,
    The lamp that lit my being shall be dark.
    I will go forth unto my resting, stark,
Asking for no caress or sympathies.

No more: for love is gone, my Love, with thee.
    'Tis thy good, therefore will I not recall
    The spoken word that doth renounce my all.
Th' unwilling doom I take unwillingly.

Yet love foregoeth all things and hath bliss,
  (Pray that the sands run swiftly through life's glass).
  The sacrifice for love shall sweetly pass,
(Doth any ask me coldly what love is?)

Love makes the way before thee.   Love prepares
  The path that thou shalt walk, and doth forego
  Life's crown that thou may'st take it up.   'Tis so
That love would have it in my holiest prayers.

Now for renunciation do I take
  My tardy pen, O Abelard, and write
  I love thee, yea! I love thee in despite,
Albeit I do renounce thee for thy sake.

For lo! I do renounce thee.   It is writ,
  The final word for evermore is said.
  (And the great Christ of silence overhead,
He keep me from the bitterness of it.)

Nay! I renounce desire of thee, not thee.
  Surely when our twain souls are purified,
  We shall seek Christ together side by side.
(May the still Christ come to me speedily).

O love, that knows no lover, but doth love;
O awful mystery of the heavenly strand;
Say, how shall any mortal understand,
Or understanding not, essay to prove?

Silence, let the long silence speak for me,
No word, no letter of thee, scarce a thought
Shall break the long long silence that is wrought,
Because thou bidd'st me have no thought of thee.

And I will do thy bidding. So is love
Made consecrate and holy, Abelard;
Because thou bidd'st me, what were else too hard
I do, that at the last thou shalt approve.

Love's thoughts are not with mortals, but abide
With the Uranian goddess and those lords
Who guard the gates of life with flaming swords,
And in life's immortality confide.

Love hath no lot with mortals, but doth gaze
Through human eyes, and all unwittingly
Doth look without on immortality,
The heritage it seeks and hath always.

Love gives and asks not back again.   To give
 Is something greater than receive, and so
 Love that is greatest in men's hearts doth know
Pure eminences where but love may live.

Love is immortal sacrifice for love.
 I die—I live—that thou may'st live, Belov'd.
 By this shall all my inmost thoughts be proved,
That constant round thee in their orbits move.

DEATH OF ABELARD

My love is dead,
Gone to his death-bed,
All under the willow tree !—CHATTERTON.

Tu, quoque, si quando uenies ad fata, (memento hoc iter), ad lapides
cana ueni memores.—PROPERTIUS.

WHY, sister, dost thou gaze so mournfully,
    And striv'st to speak, yet speak'st not for the fear
    Thy news is that I may not live and hear?
" Thy Abelard is gone away from thee."

Nay ! Abelard is more mine own.   And lo !
    Sister, I know the speech thou would'st not tell.
    And answer softly " Abelard is well "
For love hath surer knowledge than ye know.

Love needs not the frail vision of the eyes,
    Nor ears to hear, nor any clasping hand,
    Nor ardent voice.   For it doth understand,
And knows because of its own sympathies ;

And seeing, sees, yet sees not any form,
    And speaks without an utterance each to each,
    And knows, albeit it hears not.   Love doth teach
Communion that doth change us and transform.

So in my soul I see dear Abelard,
    Nay ! instantly I knew his spirit freed,
    And saw his soul's departure.   Yea ! indeed,
He called upon my name in last regard.

After the years, after the long, long years,
    I see thee, Dear, according to thy will.
    Oh ! thou art still, yea ! thou art very still,
Hush ! the great hush upon thee stays my tears.

I bring thee, Dear, these fragrant violets,
    Narcissi and all sweetly smelling flowers,
    To breathe my thoughts around thee the long hours
Made memorable with passionate regrets.

Turn, flowers, your gentle faces to the earth,
    That he, perchance, may see you in his sleep,
    And know, for very truth, that love doth keep
The red rose and the white rose of new birth.

Oh ! 'tis a little gift to give, a rose.
    But, Love ! I give thee all my days with this,
    And every thought of heaven and hope of bliss
I lay where thou art lain in thy repose.

I sing dear songs of memories that are dead,
    Great songs of consolation to be sung
    While all the tendons of my heart are wrung,
Till in my singing I am comfortéd.

ABELARD

Quae quoniam rerum naturam sola gubernas,
Nec sine te quidquam dias in luminis oras
Exoritur, neque fit laetum neque amabile quidquam ;
Te sociam studeo scribundis versibus esse.—LUCRETIUS.

Ἔρως παρθένιος πόθῳ
στίλβων καὶ γεγανωμένος.—ANACREON.

I WAITED for the coming of my love
    Long years, and knew not any love at all,
    Holden by calm Philosophy in thrall,
Oblivious to all passions that commove.

Philosophy hath cold and starry eyes,
    And looks o'er earth so pitilessly clear,
    That men have lost their manhood who draw near,
And, mortal, pine for immortalities.

I waited for the coming of my love,
    Well knowing that my love would come to me.
    My Heloise, my Sweet, I worship thee
Beyond all stern immortals and above.

For lovers know no other worshipping;
    But at love's altar tend the sacred flame,
    And call upon the well-belovéd name,
And, loving, need not any counselling.

Red lips are made for kisses, and thine, Sweet,
    More red than are June's roses, do entwine
    A smile that plays about them so divine
That, loving, I am prostrate at thy feet.

Red lips are made to kiss again, and give
    A bliss beyond recording, and the spell
    Love knows, alone the silences may tell,
For love were else too lightly fugitive.

Thine are the flowers of spring, Belovéd, thine
    The snowdrop and the violet tender-wet;
    So fragrant, that thou never may'st forget
The first words, the sweet words that made thee mine.

Thine are the skies of spring, the orient blue
    Is spaces of pure love, where love doth glean
    The beauty of the morning, and the sheen
Of evening that thou always may'st be true.

Thine is the rising sun.   In crimson folds
    Of glory love is cradled, and the noon
    Shall lull thee on to the long summer swoon
Where love nought but the joy of love beholds.

Thine are the evening stars, that speak of peace
    And rest and joy and slumber. The soft sigh
    Of the reposeful earth's last lullaby
Shall yield thee to mine arms, my Heloise.

Love, place thine arms around me now and lay
    Thy face upon my face, that on my breast
    Thou may'st recline imperially to rest,
And chide for its approach the hastening day.

Oh ! pillow thee and dream of love's renown,
    And rest securely laid till thou dost wake,
    For so shall I be joyous for thy sake,
Who with completest love my love doth crown.

There are degrees of love : and love's degrees
    Are lesser—baser—greater than ye know.
    But greater than all mortals else bestow,
I yield thee, my Belovéd, for my ease.

Oh ! take my gift. Thou can'st not take it all :
    There still is more I give thee and yet more.
    More than I know I give thee, Love, and store
New offerings where all offerings are too small.

I cannot give thee all I would.   My soul
    Hath sense of gifts beyond me and afar.
    I give thee these, I know not what they are.
Only love's offering is complete and whole.

I give thee all I can give, Love, on earth :
    Be sure when I am from earth's trammels freed,
    Mine will be perfect offering indeed,
And being completest, have completest worth.

I know not if thou lov'st me.   Yea ! indeed,
    Albeit thou walk'st with me in love's domain,
    Can'st e'en thou love as I love ?   Surely vain
It were from the young leaf to gather seed.

For first must be the budding and the flower,
    The fruit-time and the gathering and the rest.
    And after, mid full glory manifest
The light of love's assurance and love's power.

Yea ! though thou lov'st me not, I must love thee.
    Else should I die, Belovéd.   Whatsoe'er
    Thou dost I must adore thee, and my care
Is but to wait upon thee constantly.

Whethersoe'er thou lov'st me. Yea or Nay,
    I ask not, I love only. So I move
    And serve thee, my Belovéd, with the love
Not even God himself can take away.

How blesséd are the ministers of love
    To whom love yields its dues again. For they
    Have bliss for which the angels vainly pray,
Or know not in their muniments above.

How blesséd are love's ministers that kneel,
    Albeit they have no answer, at love's shrine.
    Surely they are ennobled, and divine
A bliss their pondering hearts may not reveal.

And blesséd they whose love is set in heaven,
    That dumbly know they have no mate on earth,
    Surely they shall grow holier and more worth,
And be to sons of men divinest leaven.

And only they who love not shall be named
    Most pitiably wrecked upon life's strand.
    Oh ! cover o'er their faces where they stand,
They who to men and angels are ashamed.

The nightingale doth flood the land with song,
    O come, come now, Belovéd, to the wood.
    There only shall love's anguish be withstood,
For Cupid speeds his arrows mid the throng.

O hark ! the laugh of Cupid and the glee ;
    He follows wheresoe'er our footsteps wend,
    O chide him not who is the lover's friend,
O hide beneath the bracken here with me.

Love, thou and I are one for evermore,
    Nor have two lives, but one ; and having met,
    Have one pulse and one purpose, nor forget
What hath been, nor can e'er be as before.

For thou and I, made one by perfect choice,
    Can sever not.   Yea ! even though we will,
    There is that which is of the other still ;
And one, hath but one future and one voice.

Great powers there are around us, Love, unseen,
    That every life to thought and action shape,
    And lead us where we would not e'er escape,
Though soft alluring visions flash between.

So are we drawn by purposes and powers,
    High principles and passions and desires ;
    That, Heloise, our love's impassioned fires
Are kindled yet more fiercely with the hours.

Yea ! ask me if I love thee, Love, once more,
    That so I may repeat th' eternal vow ;
    I love thee, and before thee, Love, I bow ;
I love thee, yea ! I love thee o'er and o'er.

" Ma chérie."   Ah ! thou know'st the precious word
    That thrills my inmost being into peace.
    Oh now, within my arms, my Heloise,
I fold thee and embrace thee undeterred.

Belovéd, I am Scopas, to whose dreams
    Hath Venus come in thy similitude,
    Implanting for my life's beatitude
The love within my soul that to thee streams.

And Scopas hath hewn out the envied stone
    To semblance of his vision, that men's eyes
    May look thereon for ever and surmise
How love looks unto him who loves alone.

So do I hammer out my ardent song;
    Nay! of my love's sweet presence will I sing,
    That men may know love's greatness and may bring
Glad tributes that to love alone belong.

Or, Sweet, I am Endymion, for whom
    The courts of highest Gods love doth forego,
    And eagerly doth wing to me below,
And lighteth where before was evening gloom.

And I, Endymion, waiting 'neath the skies,
    Look alway for thy coming and the hour
    I shall be folded with thee, for love's power
Is steadfast always in thine orient eyes.

Or else I am Pygmalion who hath wrought
    The image that my soul hath longed to see;
    And lo! thou art beside me visibly,
And warm and quivering e'en as in my thought.

I wait for thee, my Love, beneath the stars,
    And for my deep rejoicing sing thy praise,
    Because my thoughts are all of thee always,
And mount beyond all boundaries and all bars.

My song and joyous Philomel's are one,
 For in the long drawn gloaming fiery red,
 From out the leafy closes overhead,
His song with mine hath perfect unison.

And, Sweet, the winds are love's sworn charioteers,
 And leap with their glad burden, for the air
 Doth not escape love's mastery anywhere,
But throbs with deep responses to the spheres.

The company of lovers throng the ways
 That lead towards Elysium, at whose gate
 They only, with the master-word elate,
Shall join the perfect company of praise.

For theirs is the conception and the birth,
 The young that laugh and play about their feet,
 Dominion and all happiness complete,
Are theirs, and the great waters and the earth.

The air is love's, the tempest and the fire ;
 These all are love's sworn ministers, whose name
 Doth kindle all things always with the flame
Whose mystery adds new mysteries to desire.

And thou art love's, and I am love's, and we
  Are one with all true lovers, and complain
  That night to morning tumult doth attain ;
With night, my Love, I shall return to thee.

I count the hours since last I saw thee, Sweet.
  So many hours, so many lives I pass,
  The sands will never never drain the glass ;
So long it is, my Love, until we meet.

Now love's hour is made perfect. It is night ;
  And you, ye little loves, on envious wing,
  That play about love's sweet accomplishing,
Be tremulous and silent with delight.

You, lusty youths, hold high the flaming brand,
  And shout to Hymenæus, the glad strain,
  And " Hymen, Io Hymen," cry again ;
The lover leads the loved one by the hand.

Belovéd, loving thee, my heart's content
  Is perfected beyond my dearest thought ;
  But oh ! when thou dost clasp me am I wrought
To marvelling and raptured wonderment.

Belov'd, thy love is wonderful. Thy trust
    And faith beyond conceiving do withhold
    No word nor any token that is told
To love that may be dreamed of by the just.

Therefore I am ennobled and will be
    Made meet to come before thee. In thy sight
    All worthless—yet, Belov'd—by my love's might,
I trust to stand before thee blamelessly.

Red roses and white roses for my love,
    Love's strength and love's abiding be to her
    High sacrifices sweet to minister,
And service that her soul hath joy thereof.

Love is the strain of heaven's sweet violin,
    So played by the world's master, that there clings
    The sweetest sound for ever o'er the strings,
Love's music that my soul doth revel in.

In truth, love holds love dearer than it knows ;
    For thou art all my soul's desiréd health.
    Scarce may I tell thee how much e'en by stealth,
The love I have towards thee dumbly grows.

D

I sought thee, my Belovéd, in the night,
    And found thee not beside me. Then was I
    Grown wan with my great longing, and thereby
I called aloud for thee until the light.

O Heloise, thy name is Love, and Love
    Is wonderful and greatest. In His name
    I crown thee queen and mistress, and proclaim
Thy titles wheresoe'er true lovers move.

Belov'd, I cannot look thee in the face,
    But I must straight be cleansed of every thought
    That is not nobly fashioned, and inwrought
With pureness and with sacrificing grace.

Nay! when I think upon thy very name,
    I am ennobled, Dearest, and made bold
    To front the world around me, and to hold
New loftiness of spirit for my fame.

For there is saving virtue in a word,
    If so it be love's name is called upon.
    For with the thought of thee, I am as one
Whose greatness on the earth hath been averred.

Let Lesbia whom Catullus sweetly sings,
    And Cynthia who hath given Propertius fame,
    And every other well-belovéd name,
Dear music o'er the world's old viol strings;

And Delia whom Tibullus served and knew,
    Lucilia whom Lucretius gaily crowned,
    And every other lover's name renowned
Be lesser where love sings of love anew.

For thou regardest thy belovéd's fame,
    His only, his advancement quick and late,
    And would'st deny thy perfectéd estate,
Nor heed of holier or of baser name.

For love doth heed no name where love is all.
    (Love cannot suffer love to suffer so.)
    Yet henceforth shall men learn love's power, and know
Thou, perfect, art more perfect made withal.

THE PARTING

'Tis better to have loved and lost,
Than never to have loved at all.—TENNYSON.

Δέδυκε μὲν ἁ σελάννα
καὶ Πληΐαδες, μέσαι δέ
νύκτες, παρὰ δ' ἔρχετ' ὥρα,
ἔγω δὲ μόνα κατεύδω.—SAPPHO.

Belovéd, God hath spoken, and his word
    Is terrible to hear and to repeat.
    Wherefore in lowest suppliance at his feet,
I pray my sin's contrition may be heard.

Nay! come not, my Belovéd. Thou, so dear,
    Dream not love can assuage the fatal blow.
    I would not have thee near me, Love, and know
Thou art more far than ever, being near.

Belovéd, I have sinned. Be mine the blame,
    Who gave thee God's great dues and deemed them
        praise;
    Wherefore in the long pang of barren days
I rise not from the earth because of shame.

Belov'd, I do deny thy love this day.
    I will deny I love thee to my heart.
    And swear that thou and I are torn apart,
And so perchance forget thee, if love may.

O Love, thy name with Heloise is one,
    And breaks o'er all my vows and all my prayers,
    And comes upon me always unawares,
And all task and devotion leaves undone.

O heart, if thou must break, in silence break.
    Let Heloise not know, and tell her not.
    Perchance the love she hath may be forgot,
Wherefore keep utter silence for her sake.

Perchance she shall have peace and find repose,
    And Abelard be but some ancient dream,
    A calm upon the memory, and a gleam
Of sunshine when life's radiant evenings close.

For as the father o'er his coffined son
    Doth scatter the red earth with spirit bowed,
    And calleth on love's name exceeding loud ;
So bury I my love, Belovéd One.

Belov'd, I say no word and make no sign,
    Yet wheresoe'er I send my thoughts away,
    Always they turn to thee in swift relay,
Because all powers that in me rise are thine.

For unto thee they speed and they return,
    Nay! Love, they dwell around thee, and prepare
    An armoury invisible in air,
And ward thee where their watch fires ceaseless burn.

So through the long drawn days and weeks and years
    Thy likeness lies in memories golden zone,
    And beautifully imaged on love's throne,
To my most fixed regard, to me appears.

So do I commune with thee day by day,
    And every look and word and act recall;
    And having nothing of thee, yet have all,
Since that I have can ne'er be reft away.

Belovéd, I may live no more with love,
    Nor tread contented paths amid life's flowers.
    I wait without and know no blissful bowers,
But on the closed gate look, and dream thereof.

And lo! the gate is closed between our lives.
    Yet closed, is ever open to my thought,
    For there with thee I enter, and are wrought
The miracles of love that thus survives.

Wherefore I will my will and cannot change,
  And on the closed gate look, and enter not
  Because thou go'st not with me there. God wot
How lone is life without thee and how strange!

Thou only, Love, can'st open me the gate.
  Nor may I dwell with thee, nor there at all.
  So pitiless the doom that doth befall,
So lone the dreary hours I must await.

Dost thou, in whom all nobleness was placed,
  Most dear remembered sister on me smile?
  Oh! teach me to be patient for a while,
And walk on the high pathways thou hast graced.

Oh! teach me to be noble ev'n in thought.
  And when to the closed gate my footsteps turn,
  To be a little like thee, and to learn
The strength that is alone through suffering wrought.

O noble, dear departed sister, pray,
  If now thou may'st at all, my soul's repose.
  And lead me on beside thee, one with those,
Whose hearts, upon their path, rejoice alway.

O Sibyl of the dark Cumæan cave,
    I come to thee for wisdom, but to find
    A myriad leaves dispersed upon the wind ;
Life's riddles that enfold me and enslave.

O Charon ! bear me o'er the sullen stream,
    And lead me to the inner sanctu'ry,
    That there, at last, my mind assured may be
Love is, and love alone, for so I dream.

AMOR VICTOR

Τὸν Ἔρωτα γὰρ τὸν ἀβρὸν
μέλομαι βρύοντα μίτραις
πολυανθέμοις ἀείδειν·
ὅδε γὰρ θεῶν δυνάστης,
ὅδε καὶ βροτοὺς δαμάζει.—ANACREON.

Μνάσεσθαί τινά φαμι καὶ ὕστερον ἄμμεων.
—SAPPHO.

OH ! there are many cities in the skies,
  Dream cities of all lovers and of song,
  That to their due inheritors belong,
Unveiled in purest splendour to their eyes.

Oh ! there are many cities reared afar ;
  Pray ye, that ye may see their mystic ground,
  O list, that ye may hear in sweetest sound,
A city risen beside the morning star.

O hosts, that dwell in golden realms at noon,
  That hold communion sweet and perfect truth,
  Be mine, lost loved imaginings of youth ;
Come now in golden glow and summer swoon.

O music heard in evening hours be mine ;
  Ye companies of minstrels and of song
  Move now upon the gloaming, and along
The pathways of the sunset fill love's shrine.

The years of resolution are foregone,
  And love remains the victor. To what end
  Shall I deny my love again, and lend
Forgetfulness vain fields to labour on?

For one fond letter hath undone the years
  That vainly sought to veil and to forget.
  Who shall deny love's mastery, that is yet
So wond'rous and so heedless of my prayers?

For all men's labours cannot conquer love,
  Nor any man deny its vital breath
  That is one with the spirit, that cold Death,
Who ends all labours here, obeys above.

For love doth bridge o'er years with one fond thought,
  And calls back youth with youth's imperial sway,
  And knows not any instant of delay;
So unto me, my Heloise is brought.

Belovéd, thou art wonderful and mine,—
  Nor can the years divide us, nor men's hate;
  Nor all the church's striving e'er abate
The love that is both human and divine.

One love within a thousand years it is
    That, loving, doth deny thee for thy weal,
    And doth itself unto itself conceal,
And the remembered writing dumbly kiss.

Belovéd, now is this made manifest,
    That love, although it slumber, cannot die.
    And at the last must break all bonds, and hie
To work its own imperious behest.

Belov'd, I will not ask thee to forget.
    (Love never can forget) but to forego
    The earthly for the heavenly love, that so
The stars within thine eyes may guide me yet.

By the belovéd name that lovers praise
    I charge thee to be steadfast to thy vow,
    And even though I falter, Love, do thou
Be unto me a lamp about my ways ;

That so thereby I may have just access,
    And come within the presence chamber pure.
    Wherein to strains of passioned overture,
Love leads to the high seats of holiness.

PRINTED BY
TURNBULL AND SPEARS,
EDINBURGH

POEMS

By E. M. RUDLAND

Uniform with this Volume, 3s. 6d. *net.*

"It is rare nowadays to come upon such things as these; no litter of idle, tossed and withered leaves, mere rustling rubbish of the day and nothing more. These claim the high rank of 'poems,' and we concede the challenge. True, they amount to but little in bulk, but the quality is there. Much might be quoted here and there, the set of stanzas, for instance, beginning, 'He who hath seen my Lady hath seen Love,' a pure bit of singing that seems an echo of the early seventeenth century poets."—*The Bookseller*, Xmas 1903.

"A genuine flight of song."—*Yorkshire Daily Observer*, 27th February 1904.

"A spirit at once austere and prodigal is evinced in these short poems; austere, because the phraseology is simple and chary of violent expressions; prodigal, because they are full of close-packed thought which is rarely trite or commonplace. Mr Rudland's sonnets possess that 'fundamental brain-work' which Rossetti used to declare was an essential of every true sonnet." —*Publishers' Circular*, 9th April 1904.

"A book of what we may call literary poems."—*Daily News*, 14th November 1903.

"Several excellent pieces of work. Most to our taste is the poem entitled 'My Lady,' in the course of which the singer uses the Elizabethan extravagance with fine effect."—*Literary World*, 19th February 1904.

"Repay the reader for his perusal by many exquisite

snatches of song and many a sonnet glowing with a persuasive fervour. There are many pretty conceptions choicely expressed in soft words that seem to sing themselves into the memory."—*Midland Express*, 26th January 1904.

"A collection of songs and sonnets by E. M. Rudland has been published under the simple title of 'Poems,' and in the spate of modern poetry may thus pass unnoticed. There is the ring of true poetry in the sonnets especially, and lofty thoughts are therein aptly expressed. Verily, a sheaf of well-strung wreaths to lay on the tombs of those who 'were honoured in their generation, and were the glory of their times.'"—*Dundee Advertiser*, 18th February 1904.

"Correct, cultured, and calm."—*Scotsman*, 9th November 1903.

"An attractive volume of pleasing verses."—*Laay*, 14th January 1904.

"This volume deserves to become popular. One of the pieces, 'William de Birmingham,' has local interest, telling us of the fatal quarrel between 'William, Knight of Birmingham Town,' and 'Roger de Someri, Dudley's lord.' The quaint old legend is told with a swing that is quite exhilarating."—*Birmingham Post*, 1st January 1904.

"Manifest a fine appreciation of the peculiar glory of the late Queen's reign."—*Manchester Courier*, 22nd January 1904.

"Marked by a spirit of sympathy with widely alien principles."—*Glasgow Herald*, 28th November 1903.

KEGAN PAUL, TRENCH, TRÜBNER & CO., LTD.,
PUBLISHERS,
DRYDEN HOUSE, 43 GERRARD STREET, LONDON, W.